POLITICAL PARTIES

FROM

NOMINATIONS

‹‹ to ‹‹

VICTORY
CELEBRATIONS

STEPHANIE SAMMARTINO McPHERSON

LERNER PUBLICATIONS ◆ MINNEAPOLIS

For my parents, Marion
and Angelo Sammartino
–S.M.

This book could not exist without the contributions of my immensely
talented editor Amy Fitzgerald, who tackled this project with her usual
insight and enthusiasm. I'd also like to thank my husband, Richard, for
his help and never-failing support.

Lerner Publications Company
A division of Lerner Publishing Group, Inc.
241 First Avenue North
Minneapolis, MN 55401 USA

For reading levels and more information, look up this title at
www.lernerbooks.com.

Main body text set in Calvert MT Std Light 10/16.
Typeface provided by Monotype Typography.

Library of Congress Cataloging-in-Publication Data

McPherson, Stephanie Sammartino.
    Political parties : from nominations to victory celebrations / by
Stephanie Sammartino McPherson.
        pages cm. — (Inside elections)
    Includes bibliographical references.
    ISBN 978-1-4677-7910-4 (lb : alk. paper) — ISBN 978-1-4677-8527-3
(pb : alk. paper) — ISBN 978-1-4677-8528-0 (eb pdf)
    1. Political parties—United States—Juvenile literature. I. Title.
JK2261.M4 2016
324.273—dc23   2015000964

Manufactured in the United States of America
1 – VP – 7/15/15

CONTENTS

PARTIES in POLITICS

The midterm election promised to transform the political landscape. It was November 4, 2014. Dozens of seats in the US Congress were up for grabs. Experts expected Republicans to win a majority in both the Senate and the House of Representatives. If that happened, Democratic president Barack Obama would be in a serious political bind. Many of his party's policies could be challenged and even undone by Republican lawmakers.

When the votes were tallied, the Republican Party came out on top. Republicans would control both houses of Congress. Democrats would have trouble passing bills—or taking any action at all—without support from the Republican majority.

News flash: Republicans and Democrats argue, often bitterly. They wage hard-fought, often nasty campaigns to defeat one another's candidates. And once elected, they fight over laws, policies, important job appointments—basically everything that elected officials have to handle. And this doesn't just happen in the US Congress. It happens at all levels of government, down to local offices. Members of third parties often join in.

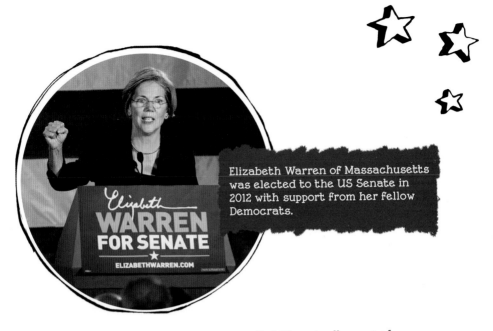

Elizabeth Warren of Massachusetts was elected to the US Senate in 2012 with support from her fellow Democrats.

That may sound like a giant mess. But it's actually part of what the United States is about. Political parties are groups of people who have similar political values and beliefs. Most US politicians belong to a political party. So do many other US citizens. Members of the same party work together to create policies that reflect their beliefs and help achieve their goals. And believe it or not, members of different parties do sometimes team up, compromise, and accomplish shared goals.

A major goal of any political party is to serve the American people. But before they can do that, they need to achieve another major goal: to win as many elected offices as possible.

From national committees to state and grassroots levels, political parties use all the tools at their disposal to win elections. They publicize their stands on issues in ways they hope will attract voters. They find out who supports their candidates and what issues matter to citizens. Then they figure out ways to build on this support and to persuade others to join them. They raise money, recruit volunteers, and rally citizens to vote. Often voters cast ballots for political parties as much as for individual candidates. And political parties can shape elections more than any single person.

CHAPTER ONE

HOW PARTIES WORK

It's almost impossible to imagine an election in the United States without political parties. But believe it or not, they aren't mentioned in the Constitution. Many of the nation's founders believed that partisan organizations could only harm the new nation. But parties sprang up on the political scene almost immediately despite those fears.

As the nation's first president, George Washington favored a strong central government with the power to regulate the economy. Those who supported his views came to be called the Federalists, after the federal government. But other leaders, including Thomas Jefferson and James Madison, opposed giving the federal government too much power and wanted to protect the powers of state governments.

This group became known as the Democratic-Republicans. By 1792, the opposing sides were holding meetings to create strategies for promoting their ideas. Members of each side criticized supporters of the other side, hoping to sway public opinion. Political parties had come into being, and they weren't going away.

WHAT DO PARTIES DO IN ELECTIONS?

The founding fathers were right about one thing: party politics has sparked some bitter disputes over the years. But parties have also become crucial to how the US government operates—especially when it comes to elections. In modern

OPPOSING VIEWPOINTS:
ON THE EFFECTIVENESS OF POLITICAL PARTIES

"Of the two great political parties which have divided the opinions and feelings of our country . . . both have contributed splendid talents, spotless integrity, ardent patriotism, and [selfless] sacrifices to the formation and administration of this government."
—John Quincy Adams, president of the United States, March 4, 1825

PRO

CON

"The spirit of party . . . serves always to distract the public councils and enfeeble the public administration. It agitates the community with ill-founded jealousies and false alarms, kindles the animosity of one part against another, [and sparks] riot and insurrection."
—George Washington, president of the United States, September 17, 1796

times, parties usually contribute to elections in these major ways:

Candidate selection. Parties officially nominate or endorse candidates to run for office at all levels of government. Party leaders—high-ranking elected officials and organizers— have an important voice in choosing which candidates will represent their party.

Message. Party leaders create the party's platform. That's the official statement of a party's goals and values. Voters expect candidates to agree with their party platform. And that platform becomes the outline that each candidate builds an individual message around. So when party members create that outline, they're also helping to shape their candidates' images.

Money. Political parties do tons of fund-raising for elections. They collect a lot of the money that allows candidates to run advertisements, travel around to meet voters, and keep campaign organizations running. Each election season, political parties bring in hundreds of millions of dollars for their candidates. They do this by asking individual donors and political action committees for donations.

People power. Candidates don't run their campaigns alone. They need help from staff and volunteers. The average presidential candidate has a team of top advisers and strategists plus campaign organizations in every state. And who are these people? Usually, they're dedicated party members. For example, David Axelrod spent decades working as a political consultant for Democratic candidates. He eventually joined Barack Obama's 2008 presidential campaign and played a crucial role in getting Obama elected.

Publicity. Party leaders help get the word out about their candidates. They may publicly endorse candidates they support. And they may join candidates on the campaign trail.

Well-known party members can help raise money and boost support for less well-known party members. In 2014, former Republican presidential candidate Mitt Romney *(left)* attended a fund-raiser for Mia Love *(right)*, a Republican candidate for the US House of Representatives.

This is especially helpful if a party leader is more well-known or respected than the actual candidate. For instance, a former president might campaign for a first-time congressional candidate. Or a respected senator might endorse a fairly inexperienced presidential hopeful.

HOW ARE PARTIES ORGANIZED?

In the modern United States, party politics starts at the smallest level of government. A local grassroots organization may work toward a party's goals in a single town or even a single neighborhood. At larger levels, bigger and bigger organizations exist. There are some differences in party organizations from state to state, but the basic structure breaks down into these levels:

1. **Local precincts are sections of a town or a city.**
    Each precinct is headed by a party captain or committeeperson, who is sometimes but not always elected by party members. These local leaders hold

meetings, distribute party literature, and organize voter registration drives. They also provide a link between the voters and higher levels of the party organization.

2. **State central committees coordinate major fund-raising events and campaign for congressional and state races.** In national elections, they rally voters for the party's presidential hopeful. An elected chairperson runs each state's committee.

Political Machines

During the late 1800s and early 1900s, millions of immigrants were arriving in the United States and crowding into large cities. If political parties wanted to gain their votes, they would have to reach out to the newcomers. New forms of party units were born. These "machines," dominated by leaders called bosses, got on immigrants' good sides. Political machines helped families find jobs, get public services, and learn American customs. In return, immigrants gave their votes to the party that helped them.

Political machines became hugely powerful. They controlled their party's nominees for state elections. And that gave party bosses a big say in the election of US senators, who at that time were chosen by state legislatures. Many people felt this was too much power. Eventually, reforms began to shift power away from party bosses. In the early 1900s, many states established primary elections. Primaries gave ordinary citizens a direct say in who became a presidential nominee. And in 1913, the Seventeenth Amendment allowed voters to directly elect US senators.

Political parties weren't calling all the shots anymore. So they found new ways to stay important. Party leaders raised money to strengthen their organization at the state level and to meet the ever-growing cost of campaigns. They conducted polls. And they helped connect candidates with interest groups that shared their policies.

Reince Priebus became the chairman of the Republican National Committee in 2011. Here, he speaks to fellow Republicans at the 2015 Conservative Political Action Conference.

3. **National committees are composed of officials from the state party organizations.** Members of a national committee elect a chairperson who serves a two-year term. These committees work to raise money for their candidates. They also want to improve their candidates' standing in the polls. That means framing the party's ideas in ways that appeal to voters.

Other party organizations exist at the local, district, and state levels. These groups raise less money than the official committees. But they still contribute to the overall party structure. In each state, parties set up headquarters. Each state headquarters monitors that state's races—and keeps an eye on how the presidential race is going in that state. Party headquarters are separate from campaign headquarters, which each serve indivudual candidates. The goal of the party is to help as many candidates as possible, at every level of government.

CHAPTER TWO

DEMOCRATS, REPUBLICANS, and THIRD PARTIES

You may have heard there's not much difference between one political party and another. During election season, it may seem as if candidates from both parties are all talk. Slogans, sound bites, and punch lines blend together. And some adults you know may think that no matter which party is in power, the country's problems stay the same. But in fact, political parties have some striking differences in their values and goals. And those differences play a big part in the outcome of an election—as well as what the winning candidates do once they're in office.

CONSERVATIVES AND LIBERALS

So what do the nation's political parties look like in the early twenty-first century? Two words: red and blue.

Republicans—the "red" factor—are the conservative party. Generally, they believe that government should support businesses but isn't responsible for resolving all the nation's

BASIC PARTY PLATFORMS

ISSUES	DEMOCRATIC (LIBERAL)	REPUBLICAN (CONSERVATIVE)
Social programs	The government has an obligation to provide a social "safety net," such as housing assistance and food programs, to help struggling citizens.	Government spending should be kept to a minimum, even if this means cutting back on federal aid programs. Private organizations, not the government, should assist those in financial need.
Taxes	People who are financially disadvantaged should receive tax breaks. The wealthy should not. Tax money from wealthier citizens should be used to fund government projects such as social "safety net" programs.	Tax cuts, especially for businesses, are key to the nation's economy. When businesses pay lower taxes, they can afford to hire more people, which lowers the unemployment rate and boosts the economy.
Environment	The government should pass laws and pursue policies that protect the environment.	Environmental regulations can threaten businesses and the overall economy. They should be used sparingly.
Social policies (generally, with disagreement among members of each party)	Same-sex marriage should be legal, abortion should remain legal and accessible for women, and some measure of gun control is appropriate.	Same-sex marriage should not be legal, abortion should be subject to restrictions, and the constitutional right to gun ownership should be unrestricted.

social problems. Democrats are the "blue" liberal party. They tend to favor more government funding and oversight, including federal aid programs.

There are no hard-and-fast rules, of course. Party members don't have to agree with their party's entire platform. A Democrat may oppose abortion. A Republican may support

The Elephant and the Donkey

Before an election, the familiar Republican elephant and Democratic donkey pop up on signs, bumper stickers, and ads. The Democrats can thank President Andrew Jackson for their mascot. In 1828, Jackson used the image of a donkey in his campaign as a symbol of strength, hard work, and determination. Later, the famous political cartoonist Thomas Nast used the donkey to represent the Democrats in his cartoons, though he was making fun of the party. Nast first used the elephant symbol for Republicans in an 1874 cartoon. As a Republican sympathizer, Nast may have chosen the elephant for its impressive size and strength. Over time, other cartoonists began using the donkey and elephant symbols too.

aid to undocumented immigrants. Factions exist within each party too. These groups may disagree with the rest of the party on a main policy.

Still, the basic divisions between Republicans and Democrats are fairly clear-cut and stable. These divisions help the public make sense of the issues at election time. Just knowing a candidate's party affiliation gives voters a general idea of where he or she stands on important issues.

THIRD PARTIES

Sometimes neither the Republican Party nor the Democratic Party fully represents an individual's or a group's political views. Or sometimes an issue becomes so urgent to certain voters that it outweighs all others. That's where third parties come in. These smaller political parties take stands that don't line up with either major party's view.

Third parties have a long tradition in American politics dating back to the 1830s. Some third parties have been very short-lived. Others have lasted for decades.

Three third parties currently have organizations in most US states: the Constitution Party, the Green Party, and the Libertarian Party. About thirty other parties exist on a smaller scale. But support for all these parties is small compared to Republican and Democratic membership. In the 2012 presidential election, for instance, only about 2 million people voted for a third-party candidate, out of a total of nearly 130 million voters.

Some third parties push for major shifts in the US economic or government systems. The Communist Party and the Socialist Workers Party fall into this category. Other parties are mainly concerned with specific issues. For instance, the Right to Life Party opposes abortion, and the Green Party focuses on ecology.

Many of these parties are "splinter" parties, or groups that have broken off from a major party. Splinter parties can agree with many basic values of a major party. But they

The Bull Moose Party

In 1912, former president Theodore Roosevelt lost the Republican nomination for president to incumbent William Howard Taft. Within seven weeks, Roosevelt's backers had organized a new political party, the Progressives, and chosen Roosevelt as their presidential candidate. The party was nicknamed the Bull Moose Party because Roosevelt declared himself as strong as a bull moose. In the general election, enough Republicans voted for Roosevelt instead of Taft that Taft couldn't get a majority. That threw the election to Democrat Woodrow Wilson.

tend to differ in their specific approaches. The Constitution Party, for example, formed from several splinter parties that broke away from the Republican Party in the 1990s.

NO THIRD-PARTY PRESIDENTS

Third-party candidates have won state and local elections. But they rarely do well in major races. No matter how forcefully they campaign, they're unlikely to defeat candidates from the two well-established major parties. Republicans and Democrats have more money and get more publicity. And they're more familiar to most Americans.

If a third-party candidate runs for president, he or she faces a lot of challenges. State laws mandate that minor parties accumulate large numbers of signatures on petitions simply to get their candidates on the ballot. That requirement doesn't apply to Republicans and Democrats. Even if candidates clear this hurdle, they're rarely eligible for government funding under the Federal Election Campaign Act. The two major parties automatically qualify for large sums of money, but third parties must have received at least 5 percent of the vote in a previous election to qualify for much smaller amounts.

That doesn't mean third parties have no effect on an election's outcome. No third-party contender has ever won the presidency. But in 2000, the Green Party may have been a deciding factor in the presidential race.

The Green Party's candidate, Ralph Nader, waged a spirited campaign and received a fair amount of media coverage. On Election Day, Nader received almost 2.9 million votes—2.74 percent of ballots cast. That might not seem like a lot, but if those nearly three million people had voted for Al Gore instead of Nader, Gore would have won the election. Instead, Gore narrowly lost to George W. Bush.

Green Party candidate Ralph Nader announced his run for the presidency on February 2, 2000. He didn't come close to winning, but his candidacy made headlines.

That was enough to get the Democratic Party's attention. After the 2000 election, Democrats decided they needed support from Green Party voters. They made greater efforts to address issues that mattered to the Green Party. The goal was to encourage Green Party voters to cast their ballots for Democrats in future elections.

THE ELECTORAL COLLEGE

In US presidential elections, the odds are stacked against third parties in yet another way. Presidents are officially elected by the Electoral College. The framers of the Constitution created this system back in the 1780s.

Here's how it works. Each state gets a certain number of electoral votes based on its population. For example, in the 2012 presidential election, California had 55 electoral votes, while Delaware had only 3. In most states, the presidential candidate with the most votes receives all that state's electoral votes. A large number of voters may cast their ballots for Candidate A, but if Candidate B tops him or her by even just a few votes, Candidate A gets no electoral votes.

It's an all-or-nothing situation. (There are two exceptions: Maine and Nebraska distribute their electoral votes on a proportional basis.) To win the presidency, a candidate must win more than 50 percent of the electoral vote.

Remember, the nation's founders didn't plan for the existence of political parties. But in modern US elections, the Electoral College strengthens the country's two-party system. It's very hard for third-party candidates to make a strong showing. More people in any given state are likely to vote for a Republican or a Democrat. Third-party candidates may get a lot of votes, but unless they rank first in a state, they're out of luck. For example, in 1992, Ross Perot ran for president on the Reform Party ticket. He won almost 19 percent of the popular vote. But he ended up without any electoral votes.

Many people are reluctant to vote for a third-party candidate. They find it more practical to cast their ballots for their second choices rather than "waste" their votes on someone without a real chance. This is called strategic voting—voting for the candidate whose views come closest to the minor party they would like to support. More than 80 percent of voters who supported Ralph Nader or Reform Party candidate Pat Buchanan for president in 2000 voted for Gore or Bush instead. Buchanan and Nader never really had a chance.

ANOTHER MAJOR PARTY?

Despite the barriers to third parties, plenty of voters say they're frustrated with their two main options. A Gallup Poll conducted in September 2014 showed that 58 percent of Americans would like to see another party become a major contender on the political scene. But one might actually already be in the making.

THE TWO-PARTY SYSTEM

PROS:

- The two main parties have more moderate views than many minor parties and therefore appeal to more voters.

- The two main parties' clear divisions on issues make it easier for voters to judge their choices.

- With only two parties in power, legislators can more easily get the majority they need to pass laws.

CONS:

- The two-party system makes it almost impossible for third parties to compete in elections.

- If a voter favors a middle position between the Republicans and Democrats, there is no candidate to represent those views.

- The two-party system creates deep divisions in government, making it harder to deal with issues and pass legislation.

Chris McDaniel, a Republican from Mississippi, challenged fellow Republican senator Thad Cochran in the 2014 primary. McDaniel received support from the Tea Party movement.

Sometimes political activists work within an established party instead of officially creating a new party. An ultraconservative group founded in 2004, known as the Tea Party, took this approach. The Tea Party pushes for lower taxes, less government spending, and "smaller" government. Technically it's a faction of the Republican Party, not a separate party. But members often challenge mainstream Republican leadership. In primary elections such as those for the US Senate and House of Representatives, Tea Party candidates have run against other Republicans. When Tea Party candidates win primaries, they then run on the Republican ticket in the general election. Still, their views tend to be more conservative than those of mainstream Republicans.

The Tea Party has a small but strong voter base. The movement appeals to many Republicans who think the mainstream Republican Party isn't interested in making real changes. In a 2014 poll, 21 percent of all Americans and 36 percent of Republicans said they supported the movement. Those numbers aren't huge, but they beat what any official third party can get. The same poll found that 81 percent of Tea Party supporters planned to vote in the 2014 national election. And unlike many third-party sympathizers, Tea Party voters don't just go to the polls. They actually cast ballots for Tea Party-affiliated candidates. That translates into victories. In 2014, fifty-eight of the eighty Tea Party candidates for federal offices won their races.

This success means Republican leaders can't ignore the Tea Party. Some have tried to appeal to Tea Party voters by supporting Tea Party stances on issues. Others have tried to strike compromises between mainstream Republican goals and the Tea Party platform.

EVERY PARTY'S GOAL

For better or worse, the two-party system is firmly entrenched in American politics. The major parties have changed and shifted positions through the years. Factions can push one party or another toward new stances. Each political race is a fresh test of these parties' beliefs and goals.

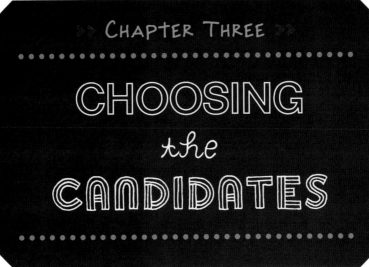

In late 2014, almost two years before the national election of 2016, Mitt Romney was thinking about running for president again. He had lost the 2012 election to incumbent Barack Obama. But recent polls showed that he was still popular with Republican voters. Those polls showed him beating a long list of other possible Republican presidential candidates. Romney started calling old allies. He asked former staffers, donors, and other supporters to back him again. But he didn't get encouraging responses. No senators would commit to endorsing him. Many of his former top staff had taken jobs with other possible candidates. As former Oklahoma governor Frank Keating put it, "He had his chance. I think [party leaders are] looking over his shoulder at the next attractive candidates."

Soon Romney changed his mind. On January 30, 2015, he announced that he would *not* run for president in 2016. Analysts noted that he had likely backed down because party leaders wouldn't support him.

It's common for high-ranking party members to help narrow the field very early in a major race. They boost the candidates they think are strongest, and they pressure other candidates

Hillary Clinton (*right*), a candidate for president in the 2016 election, gets a hug from Nancy Pelosi, the leader of the Democrats in the US House of Representatives, at a fund-raiser for Democratic congressional candidates in 2015.

to drop out. As Georgetown professor Hans Noel puts it, "Most of the people in the party are not running for office, but they really care about who wins the nomination and who wins the general election."

That's why party leaders take active roles by throwing their support behind their chosen candidates. Support usually means money, people power, and good publicity. Any candidate will need all three of those to win an election.

THE CAMPAIGN BEFORE THE CAMPAIGN

For major offices, especially the presidency, candidates start playing the field early. They won't officially declare that they'll run, but they'll put out feelers to see how much party support they can count on. A not-quite-candidate might start giving more speeches or publish a memoir. He or she will voice opinions and wait for party leaders' reactions.

Possible candidates meet privately with party leaders. And leaders talk among themselves too, comparing notes on their options. This process is often called the invisible primary. Party leaders decide which candidate or candidates they're comfortable supporting. How do they make that call? They consider these factors:

1. **Do they agree with the party platform?** Top Republicans aren't likely to back a candidate who supports higher taxes for businesses. Democratic leaders won't get excited about someone who wants to cut federal education funding. The higher the office, the less flexibility the candidates have. For instance, a member of the US House of Representatives may break with his or her party on several key issues. But a presidential candidate usually can't get away with that.

2. **Do they support the party's goals?** It's not quite enough to be on board with the party's main beliefs. Party leaders want major candidates to put the party's interests ahead of their own agendas. For example, in late 2014, as former Florida governor Jeb Bush considered a 2016 run for the presidency, political analysts wondered if he would be conservative enough to win party leaders' approval. Bush had criticized Republican leaders in the past. And he had voiced support for traditionally liberal causes,

In the years before the 2016 election, influential members of the Republican Party considered whether to support Jeb Bush as a presidential candidate.

including immigration reform and education reform. Experts said he would have to convince party leaders that he was firmly on their side.

3. **Can they win the election?** Let's say a candidate is a hard-core party member. He or she may still not get the party leaders' blessing. Candidates with extreme views—who aren't flexible on complex issues—don't win general elections. Take Republican congressman Ted Cruz. Cruz entered the presidential race in March 2015. But analysts doubted that party leaders would support him. Why? His ultraconservative stances wouldn't appeal to enough voters. Candidates can be ruled out for other reasons too. Maybe they have personal problems that might turn off voters. Or maybe they just don't seem very charming or interesting. Maybe a candidate's background—economic, religious, or ethnic—is different from that of most party members.

Fair or not, party leaders weigh all these factors. They're looking for someone who fits their idea of a winner. If party leaders like what they see, they'll encourage someone to launch an official campaign. Prominent party members may publicly endorse a candidate. If a candidate is still unfamiliar to the public, a well-known politician's endorsement can boost voters' interest in the candidate.

PRIMARY SEASON

Sometimes a presidential front-runner doesn't emerge in the "invisible primary." Party leaders may not agree on whom to support. And even if there's an early favorite, other candidates may enter the race anyway. A dozen or more people may compete for a major party's presidential nomination.

Primary elections and caucuses throughout the nation can help narrow the field. Before the general election, Democrats

Howard Dean was an early favorite for the Democratic presidential nomination in 2004. Here, he speaks to supporters in New Hampshire, where the nation's first primary of the season is held.

and Republicans hold separate primaries or caucuses in each state over the course of several months. These preliminary elections let voters choose among candidates within a specific party. They're also part of the official selection process for each party's nominee. If a candidate wins enough votes in a primary or a caucus, those votes translate into delegates. Delegates are voters who will eventually attend the party's national nominating convention. The candidate who wins a majority of the delegates will get the nomination.

Political parties use primary season as a testing ground for candidates. Party leaders often wait until primary season starts to endorse a presidential candidate. Then, if a candidate does especially well in early primaries and caucuses, more party members usually get behind that candidate. The extra support, and the publicity and money that come with it, can help the candidate in other primaries and caucuses.

If party leaders are split about which candidate to back, primaries and caucuses help them come to an agreement. The 2004 Democratic primary season is a case in point. Howard

Dean was the early front-runner in the crowded race. He held the lead in public opinion polls. And he had the most endorsements, including one from former vice president Al Gore. But plenty of other party leaders thought Dean wasn't experienced enough to be a winning candidate. He'd also frequently criticized his own party.

In January, John Kerry won the Iowa caucus, with John Edwards finishing a close second. Dean immediately lost his edge. And Kerry's momentum started building. The fourth-place candidate, Dick Gephardt, dropped out of the race and endorsed Kerry. And in February, even the head of Dean's campaign said he was willing to support Kerry. Dean dropped out of the race later that month, after losing to Kerry in the New Hampshire primary. Kerry eventually won enough delegates to secure the party nomination. Party leaders who'd pledged their support to Dean early on switched their loyalty to Kerry.

SCHEDULING PRIMARIES

For political parties, the timing of primaries is key. Party leaders want to give candidates enough time to prove themselves before the nomination is set. They need to be sure that a candidate has enough energy, charm, and know-how to do well in the general election. But they also don't want the primary race to drag on too long. A drawn-out primary battle creates divisions and tensions within the party. It wears out voters who get sick of ads and speeches. And it costs money. Party leaders would rather use that money—and politicians' energy—in the general election.

How do parties balance these concerns? They start with scheduling. The Democratic and Republican national committees suggest the dates for all their primaries and caucuses. Then each state's legislature officially sets the date for its election. Deciding the primary calendar doesn't sound that exciting. But it can actually affect election results.

The process starts with the Iowa caucus in January or February. New Hampshire's primary is next. Both these states get tons of attention from candidates and the media ahead of their elections. Candidates who do well in these first two rounds have a big advantage in the race.

The next round is Super Tuesday. This feature of primary season started because several states wanted to schedule primaries early. With the focus on Iowa and New Hampshire, they felt left out. These states hold primaries and caucuses on the same Tuesday in February or March. If a presidential candidate gets enough votes on Super Tuesday, he or she may actually secure the nomination.

In 2008 and 2012, several states ignored the national committees' recommended dates. Instead, they scheduled their primaries for much earlier in the season. Their goal was to play a more crucial role in the candidate selection process by holding their primaries sooner. This move is called frontloading. The result is a scheduling nightmare. When one state moves its primary ahead, other states do the same. In 2012, for instance, primary season started more than a month earlier than party leaders had planned.

You may be thinking, "What's the big deal?" But political parties rely on staggered primaries and caucuses. If all these elections happen at the same time or very close together, a popular candidate could sweep up enough delegates for a nomination very quickly. Imagine if a sports team played three games in one day and won all of them. That doesn't mean they're ready for the championship. Someone might get injured or the team might play poorly in different weather.

Party leaders feel the same way about front-runner candidates. A candidate who looks good at first might not be a winner in the long run. He might turn out to know nothing

Citizens cast their votes in primary elections and caucuses—some of which happen much sooner than others.

about foreign policy. She might have a habit of making offensive jokes. The last thing a party wants is to be stuck with the wrong candidate in the rush to pick a nominee.

So national committees have created new rules that punish states for front-loading. A state that schedules its primary too early loses half its Democratic delegates. And Republicans cut the state's delegate count down to just nine. Those penalties reduce the states' actual power to decide the nomination. This approach seems to be working. When the DNC set the 2016 primary dates, states that had front-loaded in the past seemed willing to stick to the party schedule.

DIFFERENT KINDS OF PRIMARIES

Each state has its own set of rules for primaries. Those rules affect how much influence a political party has on the process. In a closed primary, only voters who have registered with a particular party can vote. Democrats receive a ballot with only the Democratic candidates listed. The same applies to Republicans.

FRONTLOADING IN PRIMARIES AND CAUCUSES

PROS:

- Frontloading leaves less time for infighting within parties. Long-shot candidates drop out, and the party is able to unite around one candidate sooner.

- Frontloading gives more states a voice in the candidate selection process.

- Primary season is less costly for campaigns because the outcome is determined sooner.

CONS:

- Frontloading makes it possible for a candidate to win the party nomination based on early popularity, before the public actually knows much about him or her.

- Frontloading doesn't give outsider candidates a chance to build support over time.

- Frontloading forces candidates to campaign in many more states at once, even earlier than usual, which is both expensive and tiring.

Open primaries, on the other hand, aren't limited to registered party members. Voters are given either a ballot that lists the candidates from all parties or separate ballots for every party. Once they enter the voting booth, they choose a candidate from one party only. They are not allowed to vote for both a Republican and a Democratic (or minor party) candidate.

Blanket primaries open the field even more. All the candidates from all parties are listed, and voters are free to select candidates from more than one party. In a variation of blanket primaries, "top two" primaries send the two candidates with the most votes in each office to the general election.

Depending on the type of primary, candidates may decide to campaign more extensively in one state or another. For instance, suppose a candidate thinks his or her agenda will appeal to voters outside his or her party. That candidate may spend a good deal of time in states with open primaries, hoping to gain an advantage from crossover voting. In open presidential primaries, this is fairly common. Voters from one party "cross over" and vote for a candidate from another party. Ron Paul, a Texas member of the US House of Representatives, who opposed Mitt Romney, former governor of Massachusetts, for the Republican nomination in 2012, benefited from this strategy. Romney won the nomination, but Paul surpassed him in open primary states where he got support from independent voters.

DIVIDING UP DELEGATES

When a candidate wins a primary, he or she gets more of that state's delegates than any other candidate. He or she doesn't necessarily get *all* the delegates, unlike the presidential general election. Democrats use a proportional system. A primary winner gets the largest number of delegates, but other candidates receive some delegates based on the number of votes they got. Easy enough, right? It's not quite that simple, though. A state's strongly Democratic regions receive more delegates than other regions of the state. As strange as it seems, a candidate could win the popular vote in a state but still win fewer delegates—and lose the primary—if the opponent did well in traditional Democratic strongholds.

Until 2012, many Republican primaries gave out delegates on a winner-take-all basis. But since then, states holding primaries before April must use proportional representation to award delegates. This makes it harder for a candidate to clinch the nomination early in the season and gives contenders more time to campaign. As a counterbalance, if the primary comes after April, the state is free to award all delegates to a single winner. This rule lets the front-runner rack up delegates more quickly later in the race, which narrows the chances of an extended struggle.

A BETTER AMERICA
—BEGINS TONIGHT—

In 2012, presidential candidate Mitt Romney became the front-runner in the Republican field after he won the New Hampshire primary.

The McGovern-Fraser Commission

Primaries and caucuses haven't always been commonplace in the United States. States first started using them in the early 1900s, but they went through ups and downs in popularity. In 1968, fewer than twenty states held presidential primaries. The other states chose their delegates to the national convention at state conventions. These state conventions were strongly influenced by party leaders, still sometimes called bosses. That year the Democratic bosses picked Vice President Hubert Humphrey as the nominee, even though he hadn't entered a single primary. Supporters of his competitors were furious.

Humphrey lost the general election to Republican Richard Nixon, which didn't help heal the Democrats' wounds. Party leaders needed to bring their members together again. Democratic officials appointed a commission to propose changes to the nomination process. Headed by South Dakota senator George McGovern and later by Minnesota congressman Donald Fraser, the commission got to work. It greatly reduced the role of party leaders in selecting presidential candidates. It also required women, minorities, and younger voters to be included among the delegates in proportion to their numbers in the general population.

To meet the commission's new regulations, many states brought back the primary system. States that used caucuses had to open them to the public, instead of letting only party leaders participate. The candidate who won the most delegates in the primaries and caucuses would become the Democratic Party's nominee for president. The McGovern-Fraser rulings didn't apply to Republicans, but the Republican Party also enacted some reforms. However, Republicans still give the state organizations more freedom to set their own rules than the Democrats do.

WINNING THE NOMINATION

If political party leaders have their way, primary campaigns are short and clear-cut. The leading candidate does well in many different states, in primaries and caucuses spread out over several months. Rivals drop out when the favorite becomes obvious—and they endorse that candidate. Everything is wrapped up well before the nominating convention.

That doesn't always happen. But whether the primary season is smooth or messy, it does eventually end. And parties shift their focus from choosing a candidate to promoting party unity. This will be among their most important weapons in the general election.

CHAPTER FOUR

NATIONAL CONVENTIONS and PLATFORMS

In August 2008, Democrats prepared to nominate Barack Obama for president at their national convention. The race between Obama and Hillary Clinton had been very close. And the tension wasn't over. Would Obama be able to count on the support of Clinton's disappointed backers?

It was time for the delegates to cast their votes. The roll call began. Then, when delegates from Clinton's home state of New York were called upon, Clinton made a dramatic appearance on the convention floor. "Let's declare . . . right now that Barack Obama is our candidate and he will be our president," she urged.

Clinton's endorsement of her former opponent helped bring the party's different factions together. The Democrats were able to present a united front in the race against Republican John McCain. The convention had served its party well.

Building party unity and enthusiasm is one purpose of national party conventions. Conflicts that divide the party can weaken the party's chances in the general election. So

In August 2008, Hillary Clinton spoke to delegates at the Democratic National Convention. She threw her support behind Democratic nominee Barack Obama.

at the end of primary season, party members patch up their differences at the convention. But that's only one of the ways national conventions influence elections.

SELECTING THE NOMINEE

The stated purpose of a national party convention is to officially choose the nominees for president and vice president. The presidential front-runner almost always has enough delegate votes ahead of time. He or she also chooses a vice presidential candidate before the convention.

So there's not much suspense involved—usually. The 2008 Democratic primaries and caucuses were so tight that some analysts wondered what might happen if neither candidate won enough delegates to secure the nomination. What compromises and deals would have to be made to choose a nominee? Would the party be able to pull together?

When no candidate comes to the convention with enough delegate votes, the result is a "brokered" convention. Party leaders have to make deals so that some delegates can switch their votes. The last brokered convention took place in 1952 when the Democrats nominated Adlai Stevenson of Illinois on the third ballot.

Since that time, parties have occasionally come close to another brokered convention. The Democrats teetered on the brink of one in 1984. Vice President Walter Mondale was vying with Colorado senator Gary Hart for the nomination. The numbers were so close that Mondale needed the help of a newly established category of superdelegates to put him over the top.

Balancing the Ticket

What are the qualities of a good vice presidential candidate? Party leaders usually support someone who can broaden the ticket's appeal. No single presidential candidate can have all the qualities that appeal to voters. So the smart move is to pick a running mate who fills in some of the gaps.

Traditionally, geography has played a major role. For example, in 1960, John Kennedy from New England picked Lyndon Johnson from Texas in hopes of winning more southern voters. Or a candidate may choose someone with more liberal or conservative views than his own. This effort to balance the ticket can help unify the party's factions. If a candidate lacks experience in government, it makes sense to choose a well-known Congress member or senator as a running mate.

Candidates also take the unique circumstances of each contest into consideration. In 2008, Republican John McCain chose little-known Alaska governor Sarah Palin (above) as his running mate. Republicans had seen Hillary Clinton's popularity with Democrats and how close she'd come to winning her party's nomination. With Palin as his VP pick, McCain hoped to attract voters who wanted a woman on the ticket.

SUPERDELEGATES

Superdelegates came into being after the Democratic Party suffered crushing defeats in the 1972 and 1980 presidential elections. Many Democrats felt that party leaders should have more of a say in the nomination process. So a new kind of delegate was born: party leaders and elected officials (PLEO) aka superdelegates. Who are these superdelegates?

- Elected officials such as senators, Congress members, and governors, belonging to the party
- Incumbent and past presidents
- Members of the Democratic National Committee
- State and national party chairs
- Former congressional leaders

Generally, about eight hundred superdelegates attend a Democratic convention—15 to 20 percent of the total number of delegates. Since superdelegates are not elected, they're "unpledged" and can vote for any candidate. Republicans have fewer unpledged delegates at their conventions: about 10 percent of the total delegates.

Plenty of superdelegates commit to a candidate even before primary season starts. This support can give the candidate some early momentum. But if that candidate can't secure the nomination, superdelegates can switch their votes. If a candidate drops out of the presidential race, he or she usually "releases" his or her superdelegates to vote for the party's leading candidate.

PARTY PLATFORM

Besides nominating candidates for president and vice president, the convention offers the party platform for approval. This is a declaration of where the party stands on major issues. A party's platform can shift from election to election, based on what voters seem to want. It often

incorporates public input that has been gathered online and in meetings. The party platform is also a fairly accurate reflection of the candidate's views. It confirms that party leaders and members are all on the same page. And that contributes to party unity, a crucial ingredient for winning elections.

Platforms can strengthen party loyalty and attract undecided voters. Candidates' speechwriters base their messages on the platforms. Analysts also study the party platforms to get a better sense of the political scene. In large measure, a campaign consists of a candidate defending his party's platform and contrasting it to the opposing party's platform.

Changing Platforms for Changing Times

Elections give political parties a chance to take well-publicized stands on important issues. At national conventions, party leaders can announce shifts in the party platform. And everyone who's following the convention coverage will hear about it. The Democratic Party famously did this in 1948. At the time, racial segregation was common, especially in the South. African Americans were demanding their civil rights. And many white southerners fiercely resisted any change. For years, the Democratic Party had dominated the South. But at the 1948 Democratic National Convention, party leaders took a bold stand. They adopted a platform calling for sweeping civil rights. Many southern white delegates were furious. When the civil rights platform passed, all the Mississippi delegates and half the Alabama delegates walked out of the convention. Even so, Democratic president Harry Truman won reelection that year. The Democrats had begun a campaign for civil rights that Republicans would also come to embrace.

BEST FOOT FORWARD

Conventions aren't strictly business, though. The official nomination comes with a lot of fanfare. Party leaders want to attract as much media coverage—and voter interest—as possible.

The party that doesn't currently control the White House tends to schedule its convention first. So if the incumbent president is a Republican, Democrats have their convention first and vice versa. That way, its candidate can start building momentum earlier. Both parties spend millions of dollars on their conventions.

Major networks usually televise only convention highlights, such as the roll call of the states and the nominees' acceptance speeches. But the entire event is organized to make a positive impression on the home audience. "[The convention is] a chance to talk to people in their living rooms and not the delegates on the floor," said Frank Greer, a media expert for the Democrats in 1988.

Delegates at the 2012 Democratic National Convention cheered and held signs provided by the event's organizers.

Convention planners regulate the smallest details, down to the signs that delegates wave or the timing of applause. Delegates aren't even allowed to bring their own placards into the hall. "The last thing they want is somebody making their own sign," said William L. Bird Jr., curator of political history at the Smithsonian. Instead, delegates receive premade signs with party-approved slogans. Chanting of candidates' names, along with the waving banners, is carefully coordinated with key moments in the speeches. Each display is calculated to make an impression on viewers.

RACE TO THE FINISH

A nominating convention aims to inspire excitement. It energizes party members, and it grabs the attention of the media and of voters. All the rousing rhetoric and media hype tends to give a candidate a sudden boost in the polls. The countdown to Election Day has begun.

CHAPTER FIVE

ON THE CAMPAIGN TRAIL

During the two or three months before a general election, candidates and their parties are in overdrive. Candidates have to get out and meet the voters. In a modern presidential campaign, candidates and their running mates can expect to rack up tens of thousands of miles and visit dozens of states. Prominent party members, sometimes including presidents and former presidents, also get in on the act. They join other candidates on the campaign trail. They give speeches to promote those candidates and the party platform. And they play key roles in raising money for party candidates.

FUND-RAISING

Party fund-raising really starts to come in handy after the national conventions. Party organizations collect money all year, every year. During an election year, that money becomes especially important to candidates. It goes toward campaign expenses such as advertising, special events, and candidates' travel costs.

Democratic former president Bill Clinton *(center)* joins Kentucky secretary of state Alison Lundergan Grimes on the campaign trail in 2014. Grimes was running for a seat in the US House of Representatives.

The DNC and the RNC are both huge fund-raisers. They lend financial support to races around the country. Other party committees support specific categories of elected office. For instance, each party has a campaign committee for the US Senate and another for the House of Representatives. These committees focus on raising money for just those candidates. Overall, both major parties rake in hundreds of millions of dollars during a national election cycle.

How do they do it? These groups use a mixture of methods. E-mails and phone calls asking ordinary voters for money are common. Party fund-raisers also reach out to individuals and groups that have strong ties to the party. For instance, many labor unions support the Democratic Party. Many major corporations back the Republican Party.

To attract these donors, fund-raisers get creative. They host elaborate dinners that donors pay to attend. And they may invite high-profile donors to auctions before campaign events. Those who attend can bid on items donated by other party members. The profits then go to campaign funds. A piece of party-related memorabilia, such as a famous politician's old campaign poster, can sell for thousands of dollars at this kind of event.

Not every candidate benefits from party fund-raising. Candidates certainly don't benefit equally. Bigger names in major races draw most of the party's dollars. Newcomers to the political scene or candidates the party sees as long shots, get less funding. In the 2014 election, the Democratic Congressional Campaign Committee (DCCC) faced criticism for this approach. The committee stopped paying for campaign advertising for twelve Democratic candidates. These candidates were running against Republican incumbents in areas where their chances of winning were slim. Losing the DCCC's ad money didn't just hurt their campaigns' budgets. The move signaled to the rest of the country that the Democratic Party didn't think those candidates were worth supporting. Instead, the DCCC money went to candidates with better odds of victory.

Many longtime Democrats questioned the strategy. They wondered why the DCCC didn't have more money to spare after its constant fund-raising. And they feared Democratic politicians would shy away from uphill battles if the party didn't offer enough support.

There are legal limits to how much money a political party can raise during an election cycle. But in recent years, leaders of both parties have pushed to loosen those rules. The idea is that the more money a party can raise, the more influence that party has on the election. So in May of 2014, the Republican Party went to court to demand a rule change. And in December of that year, Republicans in Congress proposed tripling each party's yearly fund-raising limit. That rule change could take the fund-raising race between Democrats and Republicans to a new level.

ELECTORAL COLLEGE STRATEGY

Even a presidential candidate's travel plans depend on his or her political party. Candidates tend to focus on states where they have good odds—but not a guarantee—of winning. And that depends largely on how strongly a state supports a certain party.

The winner-take-all feature of the Electoral College means that in each state, the majority rules. If even just a few more people vote for Candidate A than for Candidate B, all the state's electoral votes go to Candidate A. So in states where supporters of one party have a clear majority, the other party's candidate doesn't stand a chance.

For this reason, a Republican presidential candidate probably wouldn't bother visiting a solidly Democratic state such as Massachusetts. No matter what the candidate does, he's unlikely to win more votes than his Democratic opponent. Even if he managed to net a healthy 40 or 45 percent of the popular vote, all the state's electoral votes would still go to the

Third Parties in Legislative Contests

The Electoral College is not involved in US Senate and congressional races. But it's still very hard for third parties to compete. The person with the most votes wins. And only one person wins in a district or in a state.

Many countries, especially in Europe, use a different approach. Each district can elect several representatives. Imagine having three or four people from your congressional district in the US House of Representatives. That's basically what happens in many nations. The percentage of votes a party receives determines how many of its candidates win. To snag a legislative seat, a third-party candidate doesn't have to win the most votes. He or she just needs to make a decent showing.

Democrat. The Republican would have nothing to show for his effort. The same holds true for Democrats venturing into Republican territory.

Candidates also tend to slight the states they expect to win by a landslide. Why? Imagine you have two tests coming up on the same day. One is for a really easy class, and one is for a harder class. You'll probably study more for the harder class's test, since you know you'll do well on the other test. Politicians use the same strategy. So a Democratic presidential nominee won't spend much time in heavily Democratic states such as California, New Jersey, New York, Maryland, or Massachusetts. Most voters in those states will cast ballots for a Democratic candidate no matter what. On the Republican-leaning side, Alaska, Idaho, Kansas, Alabama, and Mississippi get few visits. Candidates would rather spend their time and money traveling to states that are up for grabs.

Sometimes, however, it pays to take a risk. Barack Obama took a gamble in 2008 when he campaigned heavily in the traditionally Republican states of Virginia and Colorado. His efforts paid off with wins in both states.

President Barack Obama visited Virginia—usually a Republican stronghold—during his 2012 reelection campaign.

In 2012, Ohio was a swing state in the presidential election. Both Republican Mitt Romney *(pictured)* and Democrat Barack Obama worked to capture the most votes in the state.

All of this means that some states see a lot more action during a presidential campaign than others. Swing states, or battleground states, are the ones that don't reliably lean toward either party. These are the states that can make a difference in the Electoral College vote. So they're the states candidates visit most often. Campaigns and political parties also spend more money on political ads in these areas. Florida, Michigan, Missouri, Ohio, and Pennsylvania tend to be swing states. In fact, battleground states are so hotly contested that in 2004, President George W. Bush and Senator John Kerry both spoke in Davenport, Iowa, within half a mile (0.8 kilometers) of each other, on the same day.

Political parties help keep tabs on swing states by conducting opinion polls. These polls tell parties and campaigns which states might be tilting in their direction. This information often affects candidates' travel agendas.

PUSHING THE PARTY MESSAGE

Wherever they go, candidates have to speak to voters. People running for any level of government office must state their opinions and goals in speeches, on their websites and social media, and in interviews. What candidates say is influenced by what their parties want them to say.

As presidential candidates crisscross the nation to give speeches and meet voters, they tend to use language that reflects the party platform. They try to make a case for their party's beliefs and plans. And they may criticize the opposing party's platform too.

In 2012, candidates Obama and Romney addressed a wide range of issues. National security, taxes, environmental concerns, jobs, federal spending, and health reform were only a few. As the incumbent, Obama defended his record of the past four years. Romney, on the other hand, attempted to show that Democratic policies had failed.

A major case in point was the Affordable Health Care Act, which requires health insurance for everyone. Romney had started a similar program in Massachusetts when he was governor there. But during his presidential run, he echoed his party's criticism of the policy. He focused on Republican

Campaign Slogans

Official party platforms are multipage documents. Most voters don't read them. On the campaign trail, candidates boil down the platform's ideas into much simpler language. That's where campaign slogans come in. These short, vague, catchy words or phrases try to sum up a candidate's positions. In 2012, Obama opted for the single word, "Forward," a kind of shorthand to imply future progress and growth. His opponent Mitt Romney adopted "Believe in America," to inspire patriotism and confidence in the candidate. Slogans don't have much substance, but voters respond to the emotion and promises behind them.

concerns about the government getting too involved in people's lives. "The right answer is not to have the federal government take over health care and start . . . telling a patient and a doctor what kind of treatment they can have," Romney said.

Obama, on the other hand, defended the law. He connected it to Democratic Party values of government aid to those in need: "It's the right thing to do to give 30 million Americans health insurance [who] didn't have it before."

THE ROLE OF THIRD PARTIES

What's happening with third-party candidates during campaign season? They're not sitting around twiddling their thumbs. They're on the campaign trail too. Their parties are fund-raising and organizing to support them. And they're hoping to get some media attention as much as they're hoping to get votes.

The biggest preelection events, nationally televised presidential debates, are basically closed to minor parties. A bipartisan group called the Commission on Presidential Debates decides who can participate in debates. This commission is cochaired by former leaders of the Republican and Democratic National committees. No one on the ten-person commission is a member of a third party.

Since 2000, the commission's rule is that to participate in a debate, a candidate must have a 15 percent standing in five national polls. The chances of a minor party reaching this goal are extremely small. Minor party candidates often find this system frustrating. They can't participate unless they gain a certain standing, and they can't attain that standing without intensive media coverage.

Despite the odds against them, third-party candidates still get their voices heard. Often they'll criticize remarks made by the Republican or Democratic candidate. They'll compare their opponents' promises and plans to their own party lines. This probably won't get them elected. But it can help shed light on flaws or gaps in the two major parties' stances. Voters and the media may follow up on a third-party candidate's remarks.

OPPOSING VIEWPOINTS: ON THIRD-PARTY CANDIDATES

"I should be included in the presidential debate because I'm the representative of a recognized party. . . . [Democrats and Republicans] are engaged in a conspiracy, basically, to deny me access to the debate that's going to decide the election and the presidency of the United States. And the American people are being denied the right to see and hear a candidate."
—Pat Buchanan, Reform Party presidential candidate, October 1, 2000

PRO

CON

"Our role is not to jump-start your [third-party] campaign and all of a sudden make you competitive. . . . In sports, people understand you don't make the playoffs unless you start to accumulate enough wins to show you're competitive."
—Paul G. Kirk Jr., cochairman, Commission on Presidential Debates, June 22, 2000

In this way, third-party candidates can help hold major party candidates accountable for their words and actions.

In smaller races, third-party candidates do often participate in debates. A race for mayor in a big city may involve a debate among half a dozen people. At this level, more than three debates might take place before the election. Some debates might have specific themes, such as education policy. Candidates from multiple parties have a chance to explain their party platforms and their own policy plans in more detail.

LAST-MINUTE PUSH

Campaigns don't really wind down. If anything, they wind up. In a very close race, last-minute campaigning may make a difference. As Election Day looms closer, parties push their candidates and their supporters harder than ever. The number of fund-raising e-mails skyrockets. Party leaders rush to make final appearances with candidates. Soon they will find out if their efforts have paid off.

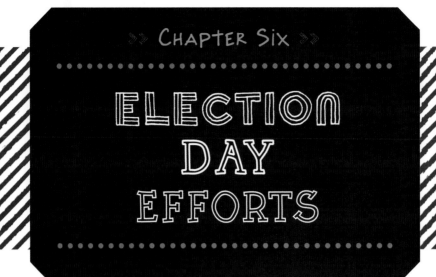

CHAPTER Six

ELECTION DAY EFFORTS

T he long wait is almost over. Candidates for every level of government office are about to become either winners or losers. The outcome depends on voter turnout for each party. Voters have a chance to choose between Republicans and Democrats—and, in some races, other political parties as well. Meanwhile, employees of those parties spend Election Day trying to give their candidates an edge. Party organizations at all levels launch last-ditch efforts to "get out the vote" for their parties. Workers and volunteers at party headquarters call voters one last time urging them to vote. And parties play other roles behind the scenes right up until the polls close.

WATCHING THE POLLS

In many states, political parties appoint poll watchers to watch over polling places on Election Day. These people are supposed to make sure that no one violates voting laws and that no qualified voter is turned away. Members of local election committees and candidates themselves can formally nominate someone to be a poll watcher. Only members of political parties can legally serve as poll watchers. Other organizations can't be involved.

On Election Day, at least one poll watcher is usually assigned to a polling place. Poll watchers generally are not allowed to wear anything with a candidate's name on it, including a campaign button. And they're not allowed to talk to voters. In fact, if there's more than one poll watcher at a polling place, they're not allowed to communicate with one another either. So what *can* party-affiliated poll watchers do? It varies by state, but the basic duties are these:

- Watch election officials assisting voters to make sure they're providing appropriate services
- Inspect a ballot before it is cast to make sure the voter filled it out properly
- Formally challenge someone they believe is ineligible to vote

Some voters report being intimidated by the presence of poll watchers, especially if more than one poll watcher is assigned to a polling place. And in some cases, critics have accused poll watchers of formally challenging only voters who are likely to support the opposing party.

RANKED-CHOICE VOTING

Election Day isn't all about Republicans vs. Democrats. As you'll remember, third-party candidates don't usually have a real shot at major offices—but in some local elections, they may be true competitors. Ranked-choice voting, sometimes called instant runoff voting, can give third-party candidates a better chance to win elections. In this system, people vote for their first-, second-, and third-choice candidates. If one candidate receives more than half of the first-choice votes, that candidate wins and the election is over. But if no one gets that

Gerrymandering: Parties Reshaping Districts

Each state is divided into legislative districts based on state laws. Districts are supposed to be "drawn" (as on a map) based on population. If each district has about the same population, everyone in the state has equal representation in the legislature. But state legislatures sometimes draw district lines based on other factors. Say a state has four districts. Each dot represents a group of voters. Green stands for supporters of one party. Red stands for supporters of another party. The districts should look like the graph on the left.

There are equal numbers of green and red voters in the state and in each district. But what if mostly red lawmakers happen to be in the legislature? They may want to increase their chances of winning in the future. So they redraw the lines to look like the graph on the right.

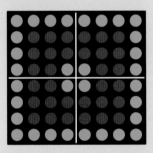 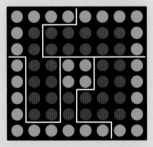

Then red voters outnumber green voters in three of the four districts. Red voters will get more representation even though there are just as many green voters in the state. That's called gerrymandering.

Back in 1812, Governor Elbridge Gerry of Massachusetts oversaw the redrawing of state districts. The new lines gave his party a big advantage. And they were very oddly shaped. Critics thought one district looked like a salamander—and the name gerrymandering was born.

many votes, the election goes into an instant runoff. Here's how it works from start to finish:

1. Five candidates are running for mayor: Candidates V, W, X, Y, and Z. A voter marks Candidate V as her first choice, Candidate Y as her second choice, and Candidate Z as her third choice.

2. The votes are tallied, with these results:

CANDIDATE	NUMBER OF VOTES
V	100
W	200
X	350
Y	300
Z	180

   Nobody gets more than 50 percent of the vote. It's instant runoff time.

3. The person who received the fewest number of first-choice votes is out. In our example, that's Candidate V.

4. Each vote that candidate received is added to the total of the voter's second-choice candidate. Remember the voter who marked Candidate V as a first choice? Her vote now goes to her second choice, Candidate Y. All one hundred of Candidate V's votes go to other candidates.

5. The ballots are counted again. If no candidate has reached more than 50 percent of the vote, the process repeats. This goes on until one candidate receives a majority vote.

The eventual winner might not be the same candidate who had the most votes after the first count. For instance, Candidate X was originally in the lead. But maybe Candidate Y was a lot of people's second choice after Candidate V. That would put Candidate Y ahead of Candidate X.

RANKED-CHOICE VOTING

PROS:

- Third-party candidates have a better chance to win office.

- Voters don't have to return to the polls for runoffs, which saves money.

- More people are willing to run for office, giving voters more choices.

CONS:

- Voter confusion about the ranked-choice system may lead to lower voter turnout.

- Ballots for ranked-choice voting are more complex than regular ballots. Voters are more likely to fill out ballots incorrectly. Improperly completed ballots can't be counted.

- People who are not serious candidates may decide to run for office simply because they have better odds of doing well.

Ranked-choice voting is not used in presidential elections. But some cities, such as Minneapolis and San Francisco, use this method for certain local elections. Third parties fare better with this system than with regular voting because they stay in the race longer. As candidates are eliminated during the instant runoff, a minor candidate may receive more votes—and even have a chance of victory.

COMING TOGETHER

Sometimes it's obvious very early on during election night who the winners will be. Other times, voters can wait most of the night or into the next morning to learn the results. Occasionally an election is so close that the votes have to be recounted, which can take days or weeks. But sooner or later, a winner is declared. In most races, candidates of any party respond more or less the same way—with speeches.

The loser concedes the election. That means he or she usually calls the winner to offer congratulations. Then the losing candidate gives a speech to his or her supporters. Around the same time, the winning candidate addresses a much happier group of supporters.

An Early Election Night

If a presidential election is a landslide, media outlets may declare a winner while voting continues in western time zones. The candidate on the short end of the vote has to consider what effect his concession will have on the other races. President Jimmy Carter learned this in 1980 when he suffered a crushing defeat by Republican Ronald Reagan. The polls were still open on the West Coast when Carter made his concession speech at 9 p.m. eastern standard time. Democrats in the Pacific states no longer had a reason to vote for president. And that may have discouraged them from voting for other offices too. Many top Democrats were furious.

Democrat Tim Kaine of Virginia gives an acceptance speech after winning his 2012 race for US Senate.

Campaign speeches are all about the differences between candidates. Concession or victory speeches sound a different note. Defeated candidates call for Americans to come together in support of the winner. Victors praise their opponents for a well-run race and thank them for their service to their country.

Party differences are temporarily set aside. "We may have battled fiercely," said Obama in his 2012 acceptance speech, "but it's only because we love this country so deeply and we care so strongly about its future."

His defeated opponent, Mitt Romney, made a similar point: "The nation, as you know, is at a critical point. At a time like this, we can't risk partisan bickering. . . . Our leaders have to reach across the aisle to do the people's work."

Yet each party's goals and beliefs still loom large. Losing candidates promise to keep fighting for the causes that inspired their supporters. Winners vow to push for policies that party members will support. In the months and years after the election, leaders will work to make their parties' dreams a reality—at least until the next election cycle.

7 John Quincy Adams, "Inaugural Address," *Bartleby.com*, accessed April 24, 2015, http://www.bartleby.com/124/pres22.html.

7 George Washington, "Washington's Farewell Address," *The Avalon Project*, accessed April 24, 2015, http://avalon.law.yale.edu/18th_century/washing.asp.

22 Jonathan Martin, "Third Chance for Romney? GOP Is Torn," *New York Times,* January 13, 2015, accessed April 24, 2015, http://www.nytimes.com/2015/01/14/us/politics/third-chance-for-romney-gop-is-torn-.html?_r=0.

23 Greg Marx, "How to Understand the 'Invisible Primary,'" *Columbia Journalism Review,* July 5, 2011, accessed April 24, 2015, http://www.cjr.org/campaign_desk/how_to_understand_the_invisibl.php?page=all.

35 Adam Nagourney, "Obama Wins Nomination: Biden and Bill Clinton Rally Party," *New York Times,* August 28, 2008, http://www.nytimes.com/2008/08/28/us/politics/28DEMSDAY.html?pagewanted=all&_r=0.

40 Louise Fenner, "Political Conventions Aim to Dazzle," *IIP Digital,* June 12, 2012. http://iipdigital.usembassy.gov/st/english/article/2012/06/201206056842.html?distid=ucs#axzz3Kg5Ji1es.

41 Nelson W. Polsby, Aaron Wildavsky, Steven E. Schier, and David A. Hopkins. *Presidential Elections: Strategies and Structures of American Politics,* 13th ed. (New York: Rowman & Littlefield, 2012), 208.

49 Steven Ertelt, "Debate: Romney Wants Obamacare Repeal, Obama Defends Rationing," *LifeNews.com,* October 3, 2012, http://www.lifenews.com/2012/10/03/debate-romney-wants-obamacare-repeal-obama-defends-rationing/.

49 Devin Dwyer, "Obama Defends Health Care Law: It's the Right Thing to Do," *ABC News,* June 26, 2012, http://abcnews.go.com/blogs/politics/2012/06/obama-defends-health-care-law-its-the-right-thing-to-do/.

50 Pat Buchanan, Nader–Buchanan debate, *Meet the Press,* broadcast October 1, 2000 by NBC.

50 Laura Meckler, "Debate Panel Defends Exclusion Rules," *Pittsburgh Post-Gazette,* June 22, 2000, https://news.google.com/newspapers?nid=1129&dat=20000622&id=S7JRAAAAIBAJ&sjid=MG8DAAAAIBAJ&pg=6982,654625&hl=en.

GLOSSARY

battleground state: a state that is not considered Republican or Democrat and that either candidate could win

brokered convention: a convention in which the nominee is not already known and the delegates must make deals to choose the winner

caucus: a political meeting to choose candidates and discuss policy

Electoral College: a group of electors chosen by the states and pledged to vote for a particular candidate in the presidential election

endorse: to publicly declare support for

faction: a small group within a larger group

fund-raising: collecting money for a cause or a person

grassroots: at the local level

incumbent: currently holding office

mainstream: accepted as normal or well-established

majority: more than half the total votes

minor party: a party that has a smaller following and less political influence than the major parties; also called a third party

partisan: tied to a particular political party, belief, or cause

party platform: a policy statement detailing the values and actions supported by a party

primary: a preliminary election among candidates in one party

ranked-choice voting: a system in which voters rank their top three choices and the winner is determined by a series of instant runoffs

stategist: a person who makes plans for achieving goals

superdelegate: an official who has automatic delegate status at the national convention and who is free to support any candidate

Cagle, Susie. "The Curious and 'Complexifying' Ranked-Choice Voting System." *Pacific Standard,* November 3, 2014. http://www.psmag.com /navigation/politics-and-law/complexifying-ranked-choice-voting -system-93837/.

Clift, Eleanor, and Matthew Spieler. *Selecting a President.* New York: Thomas Dunne, 2012.

Cooper, Michael. "Party Platforms Are Poles Apart in Their View of the Nation." *New York Times,* September 4, 2012. http://www.nytimes.com /2012/09/05/us/politics/how-the-party-platforms-differ.html?pagewanted =all&_r=0.

Fenner, Louise. "Political Conventions Aim to Dazzle." *IIP Digital,* June 12, 2012. http://iipdigital.usembassy.gov/st/english/article/2012/06 /201206056842.html#axzz3LNfbUbrv.

Fuld, Joe. "The Good, The Bad, and the Ugly of GOTV." *Campaigns and Elections.* October 7, 2014. http://www.campaignsandelections .com/magazine/2339/the-good-the-bad-and-the-ugly-of-gotv.

Hershey, Marjorie Randon. *Party Politics in America.* Boston: Pearson, 2015.

Jones, Jeffrey M. "Americans Continue to Say a Third Political Party Is Needed." *Gallup,* September 24, 2014. http://www.gallup.com/poll /177284/americans-continue-say-third-political-party-needed.aspx.

Klonsky, Joanna. "The Role of Delegates in the U.S. Presidential Nominating Process." Council on Foreign Relations, June 10, 2008. http://www.cfr.org /elections/role-delegates-us-presidential-nominating-process/p15414.

Maisel, Louise Sandy. *American Political Parties and Elections: A Very Short Introduction.* New York: Oxford University Press, 2007.

Marchio, Michael. "Lawmakers Hear Pros, Cons of Instant Runoff Voting." *St. Paul Pioneer Press,* November 21, 2007. http://www.twincities.com/ci _7519818.

Montopoli, Brian. "Do the Debates Unfairly Shut Out Third Parties?" *CBS News,* October 15, 2012. http://www.cbsnews.com/news/do-the-debates -unfairly-shut-out-third-parties.

Polsby, Nelson W., Aaron Wildavsky, Steven E. Schier, and David A. Hopkins. *Presidential Elections: Strategies and Structures of American Politics.* 13th

Donovan, Sandy. *Media: From News Coverage to Political Advertising.* Minneapolis: Lerner Publications, 2016.
Read about how special interest groups and political parties work with the media to influence elections.

Grayson, Robert. *Voters: From Primaries to Decision Night.* Minneapolis: Lerner Publications, 2016.
Learn about how voters influence political parties and candidates as they decide how to cast their ballots in an election.

Miller, Debra A. *Federal Elections.* Detroit: Greenhaven Press, 2010.
Learn directly from primary sources in this collection of articles about elections.

OpenSecrets.org Center for Responsive Politics—Learning Center
https://www.opensecrets.org/resources/learn
Dig deeper into election spending and campaign finance with fact sheets, timelines, and answers to frequently asked questions on this website from the Center for Responsive Politics.

"Our White House—Race to the Ballot": The Our White House Presidential Campaign and Election Kit for Kids!
http://www.ourwhitehouse.org/campaignandelectionkit.html
Find information, resources, and activities to dig deeper into the topic of presidential elections.

INDEX